"Immediately they left their nets and followed him."

MATTHEW 4:20 ESV

JAMES

Lessons from a Fisher of Men

SCOTT MICHAEL RINGO

OCEAN GRAND

James: Lessons from a Fisher of Men

Six lessons designed to systematically take you, a group of friends, or a small group through the book of James and then as an individual, a family, or a small group apply the lessons to your life.

Cover design and book formatting by Scott and Tristan Ringo.

JAMES: LESSONS FROM A FISHER OF MEN

Published by Ocean Grand

Virginia Beach, Virginia

Copyright © 2008 by Scott Michael Ringo

All rights reserved.

Cover Design: Scott Michael Ringo

Photo: Shutterstock

First Edition 2008

Printed in the United States of America.

Permissions

Scripture quotations are from the ESV® Bible (The Holy Bible, English Standard Version®), copyright © 2001 by Crossway, a publishing ministry of Good News Publishers. Used by permission. All rights reserved.

Character Building Questions adapted from, Neal Cole, "Cultivating a life for God: Multiplying Disciples" (Carrol Stream, IL : Church Smart Resources , 1999). Used by permission. All rights reserved.

All emphasis in Scripture quotations has been added by the author.

ISBN 978-1-7356637-2-2

eISBN 978-1-7356637-3-9

CONTENTS

HOW TO USE THIS BOOK

Imagine being the brother of Jesus. You grew up with Him, ate all the family meals with Him, even wrestled with Him in the yard as you were growing up. Then practically overnight He reveals himself as the Son of God, the Messiah. How would that change your view of everything you had ever known of Him and you had done with Him? All of a sudden you are the brother of Jesus, the Messiah. It would definitely change your perspective of Him.

Your brother is becoming one of the most controversial people in your region. He is asking you and everyone else He encounters to lay down all your aspirations and dreams and follow Him. Something deep down inside you knows He is the Messiah and that you were born to follow Him wherever that takes you. Your brother, the Messiah, trusts you to carry the very message of God to the nations.

Eventually James, who grew up with the Messiah as his

brother, writes his own letter to the church with practical advice with which to live their daily lives. James grew up with Jesus, walked with Him as the Messiah for 3 years and then watched Him beaten, crucified and then ascend into heaven. James is now one of the disciples that Jesus left behind to take the gospel into all the world. Now, in his own words, James takes everything he learned throughout his life and compiles it into a power-packed letter that leaves no room for mediocre believers.

HOW TO USE THIS BOOK

This discovery can be as easy or as intense as you would like to make it. Below is an explanation of each lesson and how it can be best used to see your family or group transformed into a force that can transform your community. Being Christians is much more than attending church once a week and a small group study one other night of the week. As we will see in the example of the early church, their transformation in Christ, in turn, transformed their community and eventually the world.

This might be the first week you have thought about getting your family, group of friends, or your small group together. This might be a transformation you need to go through alone. Or it could be that your family or group of friends are seasoned veterans of living life together and making a difference of those you know. Either way, this guide is designed to impact and lead the new Christian as well as the long time believer in a deeper discovery of God's role and plan for their life.

This guide is designed to give you and your group all the pieces to be transformed as a group through impacting your community and those you encounter. But, if you are an individual, this study can stand on its own and self-lead you through making a significant impact in your community and those you encounter while waiting for other believers to join you.

MEETING TOGETHER

Even if you are going through this alone, at some point you might get an idea of who you might take through this discovery process. You might have already figured out how and when your family or group of friends will get together and talk through the lessons. This might be something you study with friends at a coffee shop, co-workers at work, your family at home, or a small group at your church. Each different type of group you build with this has the potential to transform your community and the people you experience in a different way.

THE FIRST WEEK

During the first lesson take some time and go through the different sections of the lessons with your group and help them be familiar with each section. There are discussion questions designed for the group and there are extra sections in the "Next Steps" that may be best for the individual to study on their own. There are no apologies that this study asks the participant some hard questions about themselves in light of the weekly Bible passages. You want your group to wrestle, without reservations, with the truths in the Bible. Review with your group which sections are which, so they can fully engage the study.

GROUP HOMEWORK AND GROUP ACTIVITIES

Woven into the study are homework and activities to help your group apply the passages to their own lives. These are optional but those in your group may never have a better opportunity to apply what they learn better than taking the extra time as a group and seeing how amazing it is to get involved with transforming their communities.

We hope that this Bible study cultivates many rich things in your group as you move through the study. By wrestling together through the way God wants to transform our lives and community can at times be messy but, it is completely worth it to see our lives transformed by Jesus.

THE DIFFERENT SECTIONS OF EACH LESSON

Each week of the "James" study has about eight sections. Each section is designed in a specific manner to help your group study, discuss, and apply the study to their own lives. Below is a brief explanation of the sections and how they might be used.

Scripture

Each week of the study there is a scripture that is either a chapter or several verses out of a chapter(s). All the scripture is included in the study so that the study can be completely done from this book which makes it convenient for traveling, or hiking, or wherever you are. All you need to build a group of community transforming believers is a copy of this book. We encourage people to also read it from their own Bibles or other translations if desired. Encourage your group to read the scripture part of each lesson before to your group getting together or getting online to talk through it. When your group gets together go around the room and read the Bible part again before diving into the discussion questions so that it is fresh in everyone's mind.

Quick Notes

The quick notes is a section that may help people understand the scriptures better. They are a summary of each of the corresponding sections of the Bible passages. There are some extra notes in the Quick notes to help explain the passage.

Discussion

The Discussion section is where your group interacts with each other about the Bible passages. The questions can take your group through the three levels of communication from what they know, what they think, and finally who they are, thereby developing new levels of relationship with each other. Go through the discussion questions within your group for each lesson.

Next Steps

The Next Steps section is for each individual to work through in the days after the lesson. They are deep and pointed questions that help a person apply the lesson to their individual life. When we read something in the Bible that is there to make our Christian walk better we should learn to quickly work in the opportunity to immediately apply it to our own lives. As your group works through the "Next Steps" section each week on their own and listens to what God is saying to them, they can have a better understanding and finish that week out with a powerful application of the lesson. This section does not need to be shared with the group; it is between them and God.

Prayer Points

The prayer points are for your group to pray through together at the end of the night. It is a good way to pray that God helps apply the lesson in your groups' lives. Remember to ask for other prayer requests that are specific to the group, write those down, and pray through them for the week.

Group Homework

The Group Homework section is just that, homework that each person in your group takes home, works through, and then brings back to discuss at the beginning of the next week's discussion. It is a way for your group to apply the lesson throughout the week and then recap it the next week. It helps bring growth and continuity to your study together. Be sure to read ahead as a leader in your studies and activities. A couple of the activities are involved, so be prepared to walk your group through these activities.

Journal

At the end of each lesson is some journal pages. Journaling is a great way to hear Jesus in what we are learning. It is also a great way to keep a diary of notes, thoughts, and action steps from the lesson. Once the study is finished and the pages filled out it is a great resource to return to time and time again as we take action to transform our communities. I highly encourage you to take time and listen to Jesus and fill up the journal pages. If you are reading this in an electronic format, you can make digital notes right in the application.

Explanation of Spelling

Throughout this book I have purposely not capitalized the name of satan. I understand that it is a name and in the English language the rules say to capitalize all names. I do not consider satan to be worthy of capitalization and choose to break the grammar rule in order to not capitalize the enemy of which he is.

INTRODUCTION

Growing up with Jesus as your brother would have been a lesson about how to be a better Jew since Jesus was perfect and without sin. If you have ever had a sibling that seemed to do everything just as mom and dad wanted, Jesus was the poster child of the best child.

Imagine being the brother of Jesus. You grew up with him, ate all the family meals with him, even wrestled with him in the yard as you were growing up. Then almost overnight Jesus reveals Himself as the Son of God, the Messiah. You would do a double take and say, "Who did you say you were?" How would that change your view of everything you had ever known of him and you had done with Him? All of a sudden you are the brother of Jesus, the Messiah. It would definitely change your perspective of Him. It might also explain why He never got in trouble and was always the wonderful child.

Now, as your brother is becoming one of the most popular people in your country, he chooses you as one of His twelve disciples. He wants you to lay down all your aspirations and dreams and follow Him. Yet you know that not only is He the

Messiah, but that you were born to follow Him wherever that takes you. Your brother, the Messiah, trusts you to carry the very message of God to the nations. James, who grew up with Jesus as his brother, writes his letter to the church with practical advice with which to live their daily lives. You grew up with Jesus, walked with Him as the Messiah for three years, and then you watched Him beaten, crucified, and then ascend into heaven. You are now one of twelve disciples that your brother left behind to take the gospel into all the world. Now, in his own words, James takes everything he learned throughout his life and compiles it into a power-packed letter that leaves no room for mediocre believers.

The subject of the book of James is wisdom and practical advice for living a fruitful Christian life. James writes his book around AD 45 somewhere around nine to nineteen years after Jesus' death and resurrection. In his letter, James gets right to the point of what serious Christian living looks like. It seems his intentions are not to make one feel good about living a compromised life as a believer, but to call us to live a life that does not have mediocrity. James calls believers to abandon a life of comfortable living and instead live with "faith in action".

The themes in the book of James vary, yet, each chapter builds on the others and weaves a solid framework of how faith should move a believer to serious action and good works. We know, from the book of Galatians, that our salvation is secure by faith in Jesus alone, and James shows that faith should produce action resulting in good works.

As we study the book of James, we should ask ourselves if the gospel has changed us and broken us out of a lifestyle of being a believer that still looks a lot like everyone else in the world. James shows us that a believer should look and act very different from an unbeliever. Not only can we have the reassurance that our eternal salvation is secure, but our daily life should reflect a changed life. Many times people accept Jesus as their savior, but their lifestyle, what they do with their money, attitudes, and even speech remains very much as it has always been. As we study James, we see that genuine change comes from accepting Jesus as our savior means that all the parts of our life also change.

If anyone knows what that lifestyle looks like it would be James who grew up and perhaps knew Jesus better than anyone. Jesus would have made an impact on James from the time he was a youth until he ascended into heaven. James spent most of his life around Jesus; he watched him as he played with other children, as he grew into a man, and ultimately died on a cross for all of us.

James knew Jesus and in five brief chapters does his best to give us a lifetime summary of the most important lessons he learned while walking with the creator of the universe. As we step back in time with James, ask yourself if you are still holding onto this world with a tight grasp or have fully abandoned yourself to a life that focuses on whatever it takes to be like Jesus.

I

COUNT IT ALL JOY

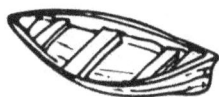

ONE
COUNT IT ALL JOY

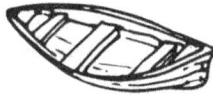

James 1: 1-27

Greeting

1 James, a servant of God and of the Lord Jesus Christ,

To the twelve tribes in the Dispersion:

Greetings.

Testing of Your Faith

2 Count it all joy, my brothers, when you meet trials of various kinds, 3 for you know that the testing of your faith produces steadfastness. 4 And let steadfastness have its full effect, that you may be perfect and complete, lacking in nothing.

5 If any of you lacks wisdom, let him ask God, who gives generously to all without reproach, and it will be given him. 6 But let him ask in faith, with no doubting, for the one who doubts is like a wave of the sea that is driven and tossed by the wind. 7 For that person must not suppose that he will

receive anything from the Lord; 8 he is a double-minded man, unstable in all his ways.

9 Let the lowly brother boast in his exaltation, 10 and the rich in his humiliation, because like a flower of the grass he will pass away. 11 For the sun rises with its scorching heat and withers the grass; its flower falls, and its beauty perishes. So also will the rich man fade away in the midst of his pursuits.

12 Blessed is the man who remains steadfast under trial, for when he has stood the test he will receive the crown of life, which God has promised to those who love him. 13 Let no one say when he is tempted, "I am being tempted by God," for God cannot be tempted with evil, and he himself tempts no one. 14 But each person is tempted when he is lured and enticed by his own desire. 15 Then desire when it has conceived gives birth to sin, and sin when it is fully grown brings forth death.

16 Do not be deceived, my beloved brothers. 17 Every good gift and every perfect gift is from above, coming down from the Father of lights, with whom there is no variation or shadow due to change. 18 Of his own will he brought us forth by the word of truth, that we should be a kind of firstfruits of his creatures.

Hearing and Doing the Word

19 Know this, my beloved brothers: let every person be quick to hear, slow to speak, slow to anger; 20 for the anger of man does not produce the righteousness of God. 21 Therefore put away all filthiness and rampant wickedness and receive with meekness the implanted word, which is able to save your souls.

22 But be doers of the word, and not hearers only, deceiving yourselves. 23 For if anyone is a hearer of the word and not a doer, he is like a man who looks intently at

his natural face in a mirror. 24 For he looks at himself and goes away and at once forgets what he was like. 25 But the one who looks into the perfect law, the law of liberty, and perseveres, being no hearer who forgets but a doer who acts, he will be blessed in his doing.

26 If anyone thinks he is religious and does not bridle his tongue but deceives his heart, this person's religion is worthless. 27 Religion that is pure and undefiled before God the Father is this: to visit orphans and widows in their affliction, and to keep oneself unstained from the world. (James 1:1-27). [1]

J esus' brother wrote the book of James around AD 45. The wisdom that James writes in his letter is a great summary highlighting what the everyday actions of a Christian should look like. Likewise, it gives a good tension to Paul's teachings that salvation comes from faith alone. While that is absolute, James reminds us that, "faith without action is dead" (James 2:17). We cannot only be content with receiving our faith and with our salvation, but we must always think about others. James outlines what it looks like being a Christian who is full of action and has their focus set on sharing the good news of Jesus with those around them and transforming their communities.

James 1: 1-4

James begins his letter with the encouragement to meet trials with excitement because they produce a firm faith. Then to let that firm faith permeate every part of you because that kind of faith is enough by itself. It makes us perfect in Christ, so we have no need.

James 1:5-7

All wisdom is from God, and if you require wisdom, God will give it to you without cost. Likewise, David explains the importance of wisdom in Proverbs 1-3, which is a good supplement read for a better understanding of wisdom. James tells us we only need to ask God for wisdom without doubting, and God will supply it. He explains that a doubting man is unstable and a person like that should not expect to receive anything from God.

James 1:9-11

James shows us with opposites how worthless riches are. Like Solomon explains in Ecclesiastes, vanity and riches are useless, James explains it here in another way. James compares the pursuit of riches as worthless as grass in extreme heat or the beauty a flower once had before it died. Both examples parallel the rich man, which can be here one day and gone the next. James wants us to understand that focusing on the pursuits of fame or fortune has nothing at the end of them.

James 1:12-15

With fame and fortune established as worthless pursuits, James focuses on the only thing which has worth in this life, the crown of life. As believers, we have to remind ourselves that the only thing worth pursuing in this life comes at the end, not anything that this world now offers. When God created man in the garden, God created a perfect place for him to live here on the earth. God provided everything man needed, and he had a constant relationship with God. Sin separated us from God and through God's provision remained it took work to get it. Now we spend our whole lives working with faith to get back to heaven, which is the place God established for us to be with Him again, this time for eternity. What we have left is trials and the timeline of life to resist our own desires and instead focus on pursuing God's desires and our faith in Him. If we instead follow our own desires, James reminds us that pursuit leads to sin and death.

James 1:16-18

James reminds us that all good things come from God, and they are perfect gifts of which there is no variation in their goodness. He then gives us an impressive picture of how much God loves us by reminding us that God made us as his first fruits. God did so by birthing us from the very words from His mouth, which is truth. We are the first fruits of God made in His own image (Genesis 1:26).

James 1:19-21

We should weigh our words before we speak, quick to hear God, and very slow to get angry. Man's anger does not produce the righteousness of God, but sin. When we get angry, we are many times saying, "I am not getting what I want". Remember from James 1:15, that our desires birth sin. We should instead get rid of anything except for the word of God, which is the only truth because only it can save us.

James 1:22-25

Here is where people get confused. Salvation is faith only in Jesus as our Savior and his death and resurrection. Yet, James several times in his letter tells us we are worthless if we only hear the word of God and do nothing to act on it. The illustration of the man in the mirror helps us understand doing so is like us hearing the word and then forgetting it. But if we act on the word of God and do what it says, He will bless us in our actions.

James 1:26-27

To make this easier to understand, if we are believers but do not weigh our words before we speak them and do harm with them, we are deceiving our very being. Though our belief in God is worth nothing as though we never believed in the first place. The power of the tongue is a powerful thing as James will explain further in chapter three. He encourages us that the true Christian life is taking care of orphans and widows (those in need) and to keep ourselves away from the world's sin. It is good for us to remember what James said in the first several verses that fame and fortune are as worthless as not acting on the word of God. Our focus should be the crown of life at the end of our life, which is eternal life reunited with God.

This first chapter of James is very clear that we have a very simple role as Christians, though it might not seem so simple to follow. To sum up the chapter, James reminds us that fame and riches are useless pursuits, as with knowing God's word and not acting on it. Our excitement should stem from the challenges in our life because the faith it produces is the kind that makes us like Jesus. Wisdom to do all this, including anything else you need is free for the asking but you have to believe to receive it. We should stay away from our own desires and what the world tries to pull us into because both produce sin and finally death. Instead of thinking about ourselves we should take care of those in need, in particular the widow and orphan and focusing on obtaining the crown of life.

- Go around the room and each person answer: Does the world's message of what you need and should pursue differ from what you know the Bible teaches?

- Are trial and challenges exciting? What makes them difficult?

- Why do you think it is important to ask for Wisdom from God and how can that help us through trials and the other instructions James gives us to follow?

- What do you think James is referring to when he talks about "rich" in verses 10 & 11? Is he talking about Sultans or do we fall into the category? Go around the room and define rich.

- How important is it we have a handle on our tongue? What are the consequences of not keeping tabs on what we say or how we say it?

- Go around the room and have each person answer two questions: What it means to be a "doer of the word"? And what happens if we are not a doer?

- Have each person give an example of what they can do to be a better doer of the word according to this chapter.

When we read something in the bible that is there to make our Christian walk better we should learn to jump at the opportunity to apply it to our own lives. Work through the steps below to apply the truths in this lesson to your own life. You need not share this with the group; it is between you and God.

- How do you handle trials? Joy? Dread?

- What steps can you take this week to meet trials and challenges with joy and use them to apply better faith in your Christian walk?

- Do you need wisdom? What are some trials, challenges, or even daily tasks that wisdom could help you accomplish?

- When you ask God for something, do you believe that He can provide it for you? If not, what are some steps you can take this week to believe God will provide whatever you need?

- Are you rich? Half the world's population lives on less than $2 per day. Is there a way that you could trim some excess expenditures and "stuff" out of your life and help those in need with it instead?

- Are you a person in pursuit of fame or fortune? If so, what are four steps you can take this week to change your focus to be more appropriate to a believer with their mindset on the Crown of Life at the end of their physical life?

- Do you struggle with how to be more a doer of the instructions of the Bible? What are the steps you can make, once-and-for-all, to know that you are a doer of the word?

- Create a plan of attack to be sure that you as a believer are living for the eternal plan God has for you at the end of your life and not living for your desires in the middle.

Flip to the Appendix and answer the Character Conversations Questions.

- Pray that God would remind you of this lesson when the next trial or challenge comes up and helps you to face it head-on with joy.

- Pray that God would give everyone in your group the wisdom you need to disregard the desires of this world and instead look toward the crown of life at the end of it.

- Pray that everyone in your group can be quick to hear, slow to speak, and slow to anger.

- Ask God to focus your group on orphans and widows, and keep yourselves away from worldly things.

Other Group Prayer Needs:

lesson one group homework

F inish this page for next week's study and bring your work
with you to the group.

- What was the last trial you had? Did you face it
  with joy? If not, how might the trial had looked
  different if you knew that it was an exercise to
  strengthen your faith?

- What ideas can you come up with to lessen the
  things you do to increase your lifestyle and instead
  focus more on those in need?

- What strategy can you put in place in your life that
  will help you think first, be quick to hear, slow to
  speak, and slow to anger?

Memorize this passage:

> Count it all joy, my brothers, when you meet trials of various
> kinds, for you know that the testing of your faith produces
> steadfastness. And let steadfastness have its full effect, that
> you may be perfect and complete, lacking in nothing (James
> 1:2-4).

Journal Pages

This is a great opportunity to journal what you are learning or the action steps you want to take based on this lesson. Doing so will keep all your notes and journaling in this book as future reference. Start by taking a few minutes to pray and ask Jesus to bring to light all you are learning and what transformational changes you can make in your life. If you are reading this in an electronic version, make a digital note and journal.

_____

_____

_____

_____

_____

_____

_____

_____

_____

_____

_____

_____

_____

_____

_____

_____

_____

_____

_____

_____

_____

_____

_____

_____

Journal Pages

II

FAITH AND WORKS

TWO
FAITH AND WORKS

James 2:1-26

The Sin of Partiality

1 My brothers, show no partiality as you hold the faith in our Lord Jesus Christ, the Lord of glory. 2 For if a man wearing a gold ring and fine clothing comes into your assembly, and a poor man in shabby clothing also comes in, 3 and if you pay attention to the one who wears the fine clothing and say, "You sit here in a good place," while you say to the poor man, "You stand over there," or, "Sit down at my feet," 4 have you not then made distinctions among yourselves and become judges with evil thoughts? 5 Listen, my beloved brothers, has not God chosen those who are poor in the world to be rich in faith and heirs of the kingdom, which he has promised to those who love him? 6 But you have dishonored the poor man. Are not the rich the ones who oppress you, and the ones who drag you into court?

7 Are they not the ones who blaspheme the honorable name by which you were called?

8 If you really fulfill the royal law according to the Scripture, "You shall love your neighbor as yourself," you are doing well. 9 But if you show partiality, you are committing sin and are convicted by the law as transgressors. 10 For whoever keeps the whole law but fails in one point has become guilty of all of it. 11 For he who said, "Do not commit adultery," also said, "Do not murder." If you do not commit adultery but do murder, you have become a transgressor of the law. 12 So speak and so act as those who are to be judged under the law of liberty. 13 For judgment is without mercy to one who has shown no mercy. Mercy triumphs over judgment.

Faith Without Works Is Dead

14 What good is it, my brothers, if someone says he has faith but does not have works? Can that faith save him? 15 If a brother or sister is poorly clothed and lacking in daily food, 16 and one of you says to them, "Go in peace, be warmed and filled," without giving them the things needed for the body, what good is that? 17 So also faith by itself, if it does not have works, is dead.

18 But someone will say, "You have faith and I have works." Show me your faith apart from your works, and I will show you my faith by my works. 19 You believe that God is one; you do well. Even the demons believe—and shudder! 20 Do you want to be shown, you foolish person, that faith apart from works is useless? 21 Was not Abraham our father justified by works when he offered up his son Isaac on the altar? 22 You see that faith was active along with his works, and faith was completed by his works; 23 and the Scripture was fulfilled that says, "Abraham believed God, and it was counted to him as righteousness"—

and he was called a friend of God. 24 You see that a person is justified by works and not by faith alone. 25 And in the same way was not also Rahab the prostitute justified by works when she received the messengers and sent them out by another way? 26 For as the body apart from the spirit is dead, so also faith apart from works is dead. (James 2:1-26).

L ove for others is the trait that makes a follower of Jesus different from the rest of the world. Contrary to how we may think, James reminds us it is the poor who God has given more faith. We are to treat all people the same. James reminds us we must love everyone the same and therefore take care of those in need. James emphasizes the command that Jesus carries over from Leviticus into the New Testament to love one. The command to love their neighbor as themselves was in the law ever since the Israelites left captivity in Egypt. Jesus renews that commandment to the disciples just before His death when He says, "A new commandment I give to you, that you love one another: just as I have loved you, you also are to love one another" (John 13:34). Jesus repeats that command two more times in John. "This is my commandment, that you love one another as I have loved you" John (15:12). "These things I command you, so that you will love one another" (John 15:17).

James 2:1-7

James reminds us that there is no difference between a rich or a poor man. We should not honor one over the other because God does not show partiality to one over the other. God has given the poor wealth in their deep faith and is heirs to the kingdom of God. God does not honor a rich man more than a poor man, neither should we.

James 2:8-13

James reminds us of the command that God gave to the Levites "Love your neighbor as yourself" (Leviticus 19:17). Jesus says that this command is the second greatest commandment in the Bible in Mark 12:29. We must love our neighbors as ourselves because failing at this one commandment is like forgetting to obey any of the Bible. James then urges us to have mercy on our neighbors just as we are free from the law.

James 2:14-17

James brings us to the key point of this chapter that if you have vibrant faith, you must also have a heartfelt yearning to do good to others. There is a difference in faith that compels a person to help those that are in need, and the faith a person has that only cares about themselves. He gives the example that it does no good to tell someone that needs clothing and food to "Go in peace, be warmed and filled" (James 2:16), and do nothing to help them have that warmth and food. He argues that the same worthlessness comes from someone who has faith but does nothing good with it.

James 2:18-26

James shares that you cannot separate faith and works. He says that faith cannot be separate from works and that we must show faith by our good deeds. It is not merely a question of faith or works, but that if you have faith, your faith is clear by the good works you do. James shows us in two quick examples of Abraham and Rahab that good works should complete that faith.

Matthew 25:31-46

In this passage, Jesus gets straightforward with the seriousness of how our actions affect us when He comes back. With all the nations gathered together, Jesus will separate those that inherit the kingdom of God from those who will not by the good deeds they did. Those that inherit the kingdom are those that feed the hungry, give water to the thirsty, are welcoming to strangers, clothe the naked, and visit the sick and imprisoned. Jesus explains that by caring for these that are less fortunate, you care for He Himself. Those that do not feed the hungry, give water to the thirsty, welcome strangers, clothe the naked, or visit the sick and imprisoned spend eternity in the fire prepared for the devil and his angels.

G o over last week's group homework from lesson one and talk about it.

Discussion

These two passages of the Bible show the seriousness of how we "walk out" our faith. While faith in Christ as our savior alone secures our salvation, we must always live out that faith by our actions. In a quick few verses, James and Jesus show how worthless faith without action looks. Even though many times we perceive the rich to be important, James explains how the poor have the "deck" stacked in their favor. In many places, the Bible shows how the poor and those that are in need are important figures in God's overall plan and how much He cares about them. Likewise, the Bible also points out how the rich might have a tougher time entering the Kingdom of God than anyone else (Matthew 19:24).

- According to these passages, how much does God care about the poor or does the reference to the poor have some other meaning?

- Go around the room and each person share whether they have had any ongoing experience helping the poor and what that was.

- According to these passages, how do you think the poor differ from the rich? Each person name a difference.

- How are faith and works linked according to James?

- Is your faith linked to works or are your works linked to faith? Each person describe how they feel their faith and works are linked.

- Do you think we have an obligation to get involved with taking care of the poor ourselves other than the association we have with their care through our church's involvement?

- Go around the room and each person share an idea of how your group could get involved ongoing with taking care of the poor.

W hen we read something in the bible that is there to make our Christian walk better we should learn to jump at the opportunity to apply it to our own lives. Work through the steps below to apply the truths in this lesson to your own life. You need not share this with the group; it is between you and God.

- Do you perceive yourself as rich, poor, or somewhere in the middle?

- Do you have a tendency to treat the wealthy better or more honorable than the poor?

- Do you really love your neighbors?

- Who is a neighbor or someone that you have a tough time loving?

- What steps are you going to take to love that person who is tough to love?

- Does your faith compel you to live that faith out by doing good deeds? If so how?

- If your faith does not result in good works, what are the steps you are going to take this week to change that?

- If today were the day that Matthew 25:31-46 references, do you think you would be a sheep or a goat? Why? Where would your destination be according to that scripture?

- What steps can you take to care for those that are less fortunate?

Flip to Appendix and answer the Character Building Questions.

- Pray for the poor in your city that God would supply for them all they need.

- Pray for the rich in your city.

- Pray that God would show you a way as a group to start or get involved in an ongoing project that puts each of you in a position to help the poor and needy in your city.

O ther Group Prayer Needs:

lesson two group homework

F inish this page for next week's study and bring your work
with you to group.

- From the ideas you came up with as a group or on
  your own, list steps that you as an individual will
  take to get involved with helping the poor and in
  need this next month.

- Come up with a list of things that you could do and
  will commit to throughout this next year to take
  care of the poor and needy.

Memorize this passage:

What good is it, my brothers, if someone says he has faith
but does not have works? Can that faith save him? If a
brother or sister is poorly clothed and lacking in daily food,
and one of you says to them, "Go in peace, be warmed and
filled," without giving them the things needed for the body,
what good is that? So also faith by itself, if it does not have
works, is dead (James 2:14-17).

Journal Pages

This is a great opportunity to journal what you are learning or the action steps you want to take based on this lesson. Doing so will keep all your notes and journaling in this book as future reference. Start by taking a few minutes to pray and ask Jesus to bring to light all you are learning and what transformational changes you can make in your life. If you are reading this in an electronic version, make a digital note and journal.

_____

_____

_____

_____

_____

_____

_____

_____

_____

_____

_____

_____

_____

_____

_____

_____

_____

_____

_____

_____

_____

_____

_____

Journal Pages

III

THE POWER OF THE TONGUE

THREE

THE POWER OF THE TONGUE

James 3:1-18

Taming the Tongue

1 Not many of you should become teachers, my brothers, for you know that we who teach will be judged with greater strictness. 2 For we all stumble in many ways. And if anyone does not stumble in what he says, he is a perfect man, able also to bridle his whole body. 3 If we put bits into the mouths of horses so that they obey us, we guide their whole bodies as well. 4 Look at the ships also: though they are so large and are driven by strong winds, they are guided by a very small rudder wherever the will of the pilot directs. 5 So also the tongue is a small member, yet it boasts of great things.

How great a forest is set ablaze by such a small fire! 6 And the tongue is a fire, a world of unrighteousness. The tongue is set among our members, staining the whole body, setting on fire the entire course of life, and set on fire by hell.

7 For every kind of beast and bird, of reptile and sea creature, can be tamed and has been tamed by mankind, 8 but no human being can tame the tongue. It is a restless evil, full of deadly poison. 9 With it we bless our Lord and Father, and with it we curse people who are made in the likeness of God. 10 From the same mouth come blessing and cursing. My brothers, these things ought not to be so. 11 Does a spring pour forth from the same opening both fresh and salt water? 12 Can a fig tree, my brothers, bear olives, or a grapevine produce figs? Neither can a salt pond yield fresh water.

Wisdom from Above

13 Who is wise and understanding among you? By his good conduct let him show his works in the meekness of wisdom. 14 But if you have bitter jealousy and selfish ambition in your hearts, do not boast and be false to the truth. 15 This is not the wisdom that comes down from above, but is earthly, unspiritual, demonic. 16 For where jealousy and selfish ambition exist, there will be disorder and every vile practice. 17 But the wisdom from above is first pure, then peaceable, gentle, open to reason, full of mercy and good fruits, impartial and sincere. 18 And a harvest of righteousness is sown in peace by those who make peace (James 3:1-18).

How we say things and where the wisdom by which we say those things comes from can be the difference between words of life or words of death and destruction. Written around AD 45 by James, Jesus' brother, chapter three is full of wisdom about the power of our tongue and wisdom itself. If we ever thought our words lacked power, James will explain how the tongue is one of the most powerful forces on earth. After making us aware of the power of our tongue, James moves on to what wisdom and peace from God look like.

James 3:1-5

Teaching God's word is a serious action, and for those that teach His word, there is stricter judgment. No one is perfect. We are prone to get things wrong. If we get things wrong when teaching God's word, we could steer someone the wrong way while bringing judgment on ourselves. The power of the tongue is mighty, even though many think of it as only a small thing.

James 3:6-12

James compares the tongue to something that can set a forest on fire and is full of unrighteousness. The tongue is the one member of our body that has the greatest potential to corrupt us and cause us to sin. James cautions us we cannot tame the tongue, and we always remember that the tongue is full of evil. There is no way to look at the tongue as something we can trust.

James 3:13-18

If there are those that are wise, then they should be submissive in their behavior, and through that gentleness, people will see their gift. Yet, those with bitter, jealous, and selfish ambitions should not talk about their achievements with pride because that is contrary to what is truth. Instead, that earthly wisdom and demonic. Earthly wisdom will cause serious evil and disruption of peace. The opposite of wisdom from satan is the wisdom from God which generates peace, gentleness, mercy, and is fair, just and sincere. Wisdom from God is pure and yields righteousness with peace when planted by those who are peaceful.

lesson three group review & discussion

G o over last week's group homework and talk about it.

Discussion

James devotes this chapter in his letter to what it looks like when a person who has wisdom from God displays their wisdom in a peaceful, gentle, merciful, fair, just and sincere way. This wise person bridles their tongue, is slow to speak, and uses their gift of pure wisdom by yielding righteousness with peace when planted.

- According to James 3, how powerful is the tongue?

- Go around the room and give an example, like James does the rudder, of a small physical object that controls a large object.

- Give examples of how evil the tongue is, full of poison and unrighteousness.

- Do you think the tongue in has become more evil, less evil or about the same as when James wrote his letter in A.D. 45? Why?

- Do you think Christians are better at controlling their tongue and thus producing better "fruit" than the rest of the world?

- Go around the room and explain the situation you

find yourself in where it is most difficult to "hold your tongue" and why.

- Why are jealousy and selfish ambition in your own life opposite to the wisdom of God?

- What are some ways that you can use God's pure wisdom and yield righteousness sown in peace (bridling your tongue and body) when you find yourself in a situation that tempts you to do otherwise?

lesson three next steps

W hen we read something in the bible that is there to make our Christian walk better we should learn to jump at the opportunity to apply it to our own lives. Work through the steps below to apply the truths in this lesson to your own life. You need not share this with the group; it is between you and God.

- When you read James 3, how are you convicted in the way you guide your body with your tongue?

- Thinking back over your life list four times when you have used your tongue to curse people and tainted your entire body.

- List three people that come to mind when you read, "By his good conduct let him show his works in the meekness of wisdom" (James 3:13).

- List three areas where you struggle with jealousy and selfish ambition.

- Write 4 steps you are going to take this week to

move toward being more peaceable, gentle, open to reason, full of mercy and good fruits, impartial, and sincere.

- Brainstorm and come up with two personal methods that you can put in place that will trigger you to make peace and show your gentleness in situations where you might usually allow your tongue to be unrighteous.

- Take a moment and ask God to take away any jealousy and selfish ambition and to replace it instead with His pure wisdom and peace so that you can yield a harvest of righteousness.

- Pray that God would help you and those in your group to control your tongues and only sow peace with them.

- Pray that your life motives would be free from jealousy and selfish ambition.

- Pray for peace in the world.

Other Group Prayer Needs:

lesson three group homework

F inish this page for next week's study and bring your work with you to group.

- Write a paragraph about a time your tongue got you in the most trouble and, "set a forest ablaze" (James 3:5). Be honest about the details.

- With your paragraph written, write a scene as though it happened, had you instead been peaceable, gentle, open to reason, full of mercy and good fruits, impartial, and sincere in the situation. Make-believe you did the right thing and show how good fruits can come from the same situation.

Memorize this passage:

But the wisdom from above is first pure, then peaceable, gentle, open to reason, full of mercy and good fruits, impartial and sincere. 18 And a harvest of righteousness is sown in peace by those who make peace (James 3:17 & 18)

Journal Pages

This is a great opportunity to journal what you are learning or the action steps you want to take based on this lesson. Doing so will keep all your notes and journaling in this book as future reference. Start by taking a few minutes to pray and ask Jesus to bring to light all you are learning and what transformational changes you can make in your life. If you are reading this in an electronic version, make a digital note and journal.

Journal Pages

IV

QUARRELS

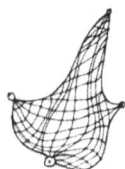

FOUR
QUARRELS

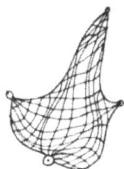

James 4:1-17

Warning Against Worldliness

1 What causes quarrels and what causes fights among you? Is it not this, that your passions are at war within you? 2 You desire and do not have, so you murder. You covet and cannot obtain, so you fight and quarrel. You do not have, because you do not ask. 3 You ask and do not receive, because you ask wrongly, to spend it on your passions. 4 You adulterous people! Do you not know that friendship with the world is enmity with God? Therefore whoever wishes to be a friend of the world makes himself an enemy of God. 5 Or do you suppose it is to no purpose that the Scripture says, "He yearns jealously over the spirit that he has made to dwell in us"? 6 But he gives more grace. Therefore it says, "God opposes the proud but gives grace to the humble." 7 Submit yourselves therefore to God. Resist the devil, and he will flee from you. 8 Draw near to God, and he will draw

near to you. Cleanse your hands, you sinners, and purify your hearts, you double-minded. 9 Be wretched and mourn and weep. Let your laughter be turned to mourning and your joy to gloom. 10 Humble yourselves before the Lord, and he will exalt you.

11 Do not speak evil against one another, brothers. The one who speaks against a brother or judges his brother, speaks evil against the law and judges the law. But if you judge the law, you are not a doer of the law but a judge. 12 There is only one lawgiver and judge, he who is able to save and to destroy. But who are you to judge your neighbor?

Boasting About Tomorrow

13 Come now, you who say, "Today or tomorrow we will go into such and such a town and spend a year there and trade and make a profit"—14 yet you do not know what tomorrow will bring. What is your life? For you are a mist that appears for a little time and then vanishes. 15 Instead you ought to say, "If the Lord wills, we will live and do this or that." 16 As it is, you boast in your arrogance. All such boasting is evil. 17 So whoever knows the right thing to do and fails to do it, for him it is sin (James 4:1-17).

In chapter 4, James digs in a little deeper about how we treat each other and what we place our life focus on. There is no mincing of words with James being very blunt about petty arguments. It closely relates chapter four to the first chapter, as if he expounded a little more on some points he made there. Remember, James is writing to an audience that has serious divisions happening in the church. His themes in this chapter are the selfishness of quarrels, talking badly about each other, and reminding there is no promise of tomorrow.

James 4:1-10

Quarrels are a common thing in humanity. Yet, James points out that they should be rare among believers. James points to the fact that our quarrels arise because we desire something we do not have. Remember from James 1:15 that our desires give birth to sin, and sin, death. Instead, all we have to do is ask God for what we need, and if we need it, He will supply it. James hits the nail on the head when he explains that we many times ask God for something with the wrong intention of its use when we ask. James is reminding us again, like in Chapter 1, when we get in quarrels we are many times saying, "I am not getting what I want". Yet, God is your provider, not others, He will supply what you need when you ask for it in the right ways and intentions.

James reminds us that association with the world is the opposite of being close to God, that association with the world makes you an enemy of God. God has an intense desire to hold on to the spirit that He made to dwell in each one of us. God gives us the grace that we need to resist the world and satan so we can keep from temptations or associated with worldly things. If we seek God with all our hearts, then He will be right beside us. Again James urges us to let go of all worldly sin and find unity with joy to God. If we come to God; understanding that we are not the important ones, and He is God, He will exalt us.

James 4:11-12

In chapter 3 James was very clear about the power of the tongue and now reminds us how to control it. Not only is the tongue, as James explained in chapter 3, a world of unrighteousness; we are not to use it to speak with evil against others. By speaking against others, we also judge the law becoming like one who draws up laws. We must remember there is only one who has the authority to make laws, God, and we must never exalt ourselves toward being equal with God. Speaking against a brother is not only something that affects them, but also our relationship with God.

James 4:13-17

Even as believers God never promises us tomorrow. James reminds us we are each only here a little while. To make plans and boast about them is foolish and arrogant. Instead, we should listen to what God tells us to do today and do it, that way we can do God's will for us as He reveals it to us. Otherwise, failure at the mission He gives us and instead engage in plans for what we will do tomorrow is a sin.

lesson four group review & discussion

G o over last week's group homework and talk about it.

Discussion

In chapter 4, James covers topics that are vital that we understand and make a part of our daily lives as believers. It is important as believers that we are solid in our knowledge that our
provision comes from God, not from each other. Likewise, we
are mere humans and should never think we are any better
than we are. We do not determine the law or what will come
tomorrow. Instead, like James tells us in chapter 1, our focus
should be the crown of life at the end of our life, which is
eternal life reunited with God.

- Go around the room and each person answer "Do
  fights and quarrels develop from people wanting
  something that they do not have?" (I'm not getting
  what I want!)

- Is it possible to associate with things of the world
  and maintain a right relationship with God at the
  same time?

- Where do you think the "line" is between being in
  the world but not being of the world?

- Each person in the group name the reason you find
  yourself in a quarrel or fight the most often? Is the
  reason linked to your desires?

- Go around the room and each person describe several things people do to plan for the future because they think tomorrow is a given. Discuss why James says that is that evil.

- For each person in the group, is God's will the first thing you think about when you're making plans for tomorrow or the future? Why is it important, according to James, to keep God's will forefront when making plans?

- What are some ideas of things you can do to make sure you are not engaged in the world and instead put God's priorities and will first when making plans for the future? How might believers be more counter-cultural?

- Go around the room and each person give an example of when your desires can put you in a bad spot?

W hen we read something in the bible that is there to make our Christian walk better we should learn to jump at the opportunity to apply it to our own lives. Work through the steps below to apply the truths in this lesson to your own life. You need not share this with the group; it is between you and God.

- Do your desires of the things you do not have cause you to quarrel and fight with others, your spouse, your roommate?

- When you ask God for things or provision, do you ask Him with the actual intention of using it for His glory?

- In what areas in your life are you going to work a lot harder to stay disengaged from worldly things? Write the areas down, then write four things you can do this week to become completely disengaged with them. It is wise to find an accountability partner to keep each other in check.

- Do you speak against others frequently? If so, what

are the steps you are going to take to become better
at not speaking against them?

- What is it going to take for you to stop having a
  friendship with the world and instead be an ally of
  God's? Write the steps you will take this week.

- Are you a proud person, having or showing a high
  or excessively high opinion of oneself or one's
  importance? Are you willing to follow the
  directions in James 4:6-10 so He can exalt you?

- Do you believe that you spend too much time
  planning your life out for the future and not
  enough time listening to God about what you can
  do to fulfill His will in your life today? Spend the
  next day listening to God and write down the plans
  He wants you to finish for Him and see how those
  compare to what you had planned out.

- Do you include listening to God in all the plans
  you make for the future? What steps can you take
  beginning this week to include God in all your
  plans, both for today and onward?

Flip to the Appendix and answer the Character Conversations Questions

- Pray that God will help the members of your group not quarrel or fight within your group or with those outside of it.

- Pray that God will empower the members of your group and yourself to resist worldly things.

- Pray for you and the members of your group that you can live humble and pure lives before God, so He can exalt you.

Other Group Prayer Needs:

F inish this page for next week's study and bring your work with you to group.

- How do you handle quarrels and disagreements when you get in them? Explain your last quarrel and if involved in it was something you desired but did not have. How might the last quarrel looked different had you taken what you desired out of it?

- What ideas can you come up with in your own life to keep you less in association with the world and instead, walking in God's grace to resist the world? Write three examples of what you do now and how you could change that to resist the world more.

- What kind of system or strategy can you think of that you and others could put in place to focus on what God is telling you to do today with your life and less engaged with what you are doing to secure promises for tomorrow? Write it down here to share it with the group.

Memorize this passage:

But he gives more grace. Therefore it says, "God opposes the proud, but gives grace to the humble." Submit yourselves therefore to God. Resist the devil, and he will flee from you. Draw near to God, and he will draw near to you. Cleanse your hands, you sinners, and purify your hearts, you double-minded. Be wretched and mourn and weep. Let your laughter be turned to mourning and your joy to gloom. Humble yourselves before the Lord, and he will exalt you (James 4:6-10).

Journal Pages

This is a great opportunity to journal what you are learning or the action steps you want to take based on this lesson. Doing so will keep all your notes and journaling in this book as future reference. Start by taking a few minutes to pray and ask Jesus to bring to light all you are learning and what transformational changes you can make in your life. If you are reading this in an electronic version, make a digital note and journal.

Journal Pages

V
_____

"YES" AND "NO"

FIVE
"YES" AND "NO"

Jame 5:1-20

Warning to the Rich

1 Come now, you rich, weep and howl for the miseries that are coming upon you. 2 Your riches have rotted and your garments are moth-eaten. 3 Your gold and silver have corroded, and their corrosion will be evidence against you and will eat your flesh like fire. You have laid up treasure in the last days. 4 Behold, the wages of the laborers who mowed your fields, which you kept back by fraud, are crying out against you, and the cries of the harvesters have reached the ears of the Lord of hosts. 5 You have lived on the earth in luxury and in self-indulgence. You have fattened your hearts in a day of slaughter. 6 You have condemned and murdered the righteous person. He does not resist you.

Patience in Suffering

7 Be patient, therefore, brothers, until the coming of the

Lord. See how the farmer waits for the precious fruit of the earth, being patient about it, until it receives the early and the late rains. 8 You also, be patient. Establish your hearts, for the coming of the Lord is at hand. 9 Do not grumble against one another, brothers, so that you may not be judged; behold, the Judge is standing at the door. 10 As an example of suffering and patience, brothers, take the prophets who spoke in the name of the Lord. 11 Behold, we consider those blessed who remained steadfast. You have heard of the steadfastness of Job, and you have seen the purpose of the Lord, how the Lord is compassionate and merciful.

12 But above all, my brothers, do not swear, either by heaven or by earth or by any other oath, but let your "yes" be yes and your "no" be no, so that you may not fall under condemnation.

The Prayer of Faith

13 Is anyone among you suffering? Let him pray. Is anyone cheerful? Let him sing praise. 14 Is anyone among you sick? Let him call for the elders of the church, and let them pray over him, anointing him with oil in the name of the Lord. 15 And the prayer of faith will save the one who is sick, and the Lord will raise him up. And if he has committed sins, he will be forgiven. 16 Therefore, confess your sins to one another and pray for one another, that you may be healed. The prayer of a righteous person has great power as it is working. 17 Elijah was a man with a nature like ours, and he prayed fervently that it might not rain, and for three years and six months it did not rain on the earth. 18 Then he prayed again, and heaven gave rain, and the earth bore its fruit.

19 My brothers, if anyone among you wanders from the truth and someone brings him back, 20 let him know that whoever brings back a sinner from his wandering will save his soul from death and will cover a multitude of sins (James 5:1-20).

A s James finishes up his letter, he returns once again to remind those that live in luxury and hoarded up riches that the day is coming where riches will be nothing. As James explains, those riches even will turn against them. He closes his letter with encouragement to believers to be patient and steadfast even when facing difficulty, and gives some practical spiritual advice that can help in the time of trouble.

James 5:1-6

Once again James focuses on the rich and reminds us that discomfort is coming for them because their wealth will be a judgment against them. In fact, their wealth and anyone they deceived to get the wealth will turn against them on the day of judgment. Storing up wealth has fattened their hearts for a cruel and violent death.

James 5:7-11

James encourages believers to be patient like the farmer who waits for rain by firming up their hearts for Jesus' coming. He reminds us not to complain or be bad-tempered to one another. Instead, we are to remember those who went before us that was an example of how to act in suffering and patience. James reminds us of Job, who was unwavering and God had compassion for him.

James 5:12

James urges us that we stay true to when we say "yes and no." As believers, we should not have to add a "tag line" or a guarantee that makes us any more believable. James warns that if our "yes" and "no" cannot be exactly that, we force people to see us as undesirable.

James 5:13-18

James gives us practical advice on meeting specific needs, that we should pray when we are suffering and sing when we are cheerful. Likewise, if we are sick, we should ask the elders of our church to anoint us with oil and pray for us in the name of Jesus. It is through faith when we pray that God will make us well when we are sick and forgive our sins. We must be accountable to each other and share the areas where we are having trouble with sin. There is power in praying for each other in the areas of our challenges. Working together and praying for each other produces excellent results. If we doubt that, James reminds us of the faith in prayer that Elijah had.

James 5:19-20

The Bible teaches in many places we stay involved in each other's lives. When another believer strays from the Bible truths, we should care and do everything we can to help them turn back to Jesus and the truth. When we care and get involved with helping others come back to the truth, we help save them from death. It matters.

lesson five group review & discussion

G o over last week's group homework from lesson four and
talk about it.

Discussion

As James closes his letter, he gives us some warning and great
practical applications to work on. We as believers need to be
careful as we continue our walk, we pay close attention to the
instruction in this chapter as James prepares us for blessings
and challenges.

- What are all the things you know, from the study of
  James, about the warnings he gives to the rich?

- What have you learned, from the study of James,
  about persevering through trials and having faith
  until Jesus comes back?

- Who do you think James is talking to in verses 1-6?
  From everything else you have studied in James,
  who do you think the "rich" are that James is
  warning?

- Go around the room and describe how society's
  "yes" and "no" lack integrity.

- What are the similarities in James 5:13-18 and
  James 1?

- How can you be more proactive in "bringing back sinners from their wanderings?"

- What is the section, truth or warning of James 5 that stands out the most to you? Why?

- Go around the room and give a 1 minute summary of the book of James and what you learned.

W hen we read something in the bible that is there to make our Christian walk better we should learn to jump at the opportunity to apply it to our own lives. Work through the steps below to apply the truths in this lesson to your own life. You need not share this with the group; it is between you and God.

- What part of your life are you convicted about when you read James 5:1-6? What can step can you take this week so that when you read James 5:1-6 you no longer feel convicted?

- How might God see you as living in luxury and self-indulgence? How could you restructure your life so that God sees you living more within necessities and focused on others instead of yourself?

- How might James's words "Do not grumble against one another, brothers, so that you may not be judged" (James 5:9) apply to you?

- What four steps can you put in place this week so

you will catch yourself when you grumble with another?

- What are two examples where your "yes" has not been yes or your "no" not been no? How can you strengthen your integrity so much that when you say "yes" or "no" people know you mean it?

- Do you pray when you are suffering? Do you sing when you are cheerful? Do you ask other believers to pray for you when you are sick? If your answer to any of these is no, then what can you do to make sure you follow this advice from James?

- Do you have someone in your life that you are accountable to and meet with from now on to keep you spiritually in check? If not, come up with the names of two people that you could ask this week to be that accountability for you.

- Who do you know that you could get involved with whom is wandering from the truth? What are some ways that you could turn that person around to the gospel?

Flip to the Appendix and answer the Character Conversations Questions.

- Pray that you and those in your group will use the money God provides you with to glorifying God and His purposes instead of storing it up or living in luxury or self- indulgence.

- Pray that God will grant everyone in your group patience and help you stay steadfast in faith until Jesus comes back.

- Pray that God will help you guard yourselves against grumbling against one another.

- Pray that God will empower you to make your "yes" be yes and your "no" be no.

- Pray for the sick in your church.

- Pray that God will help you be passionate about

those that have gone astray and that He would put them in your path to guide back to the truth.

Other Group Prayer Needs:

F inish this page for next week's study and bring your work with you to group.

- What are three situations where you find it toughest to have patience? Come up with three things you could do for each to have more patience when those situations arise.

- Come up with two ideas that you could put in place this week that would keep you on the lookout for those that are wandering away from God.

Memorize this passage:

My brothers, if anyone among you wanders from the truth and someone brings him back, let him know that whoever brings back a sinner from his wandering will save his soul from death and will cover a multitude of sins (James 5:19 & 20).

Journal Pages

This is a great opportunity to journal what you are learning or the action steps you want to take based on this lesson. Doing so will keep all your notes and journaling in this book as future reference. Start by taking a few minutes to pray and ask Jesus to bring to light all you are learning and what transformational changes you can make in your life. If you are reading this in an electronic version, make a digital note and journal.

_____

_____

_____

_____

_____

_____

_____

_____

_____

_____

_____

_____

_____

_____

_____

_____

_____

_____

_____

_____

_____

_____

_____

_____

Journal Pages

APPENDIX

Character Building Questions

The best way to use these questions is to pick the same-gender partner to be accountable to each week. By asking each other these questions you can stay accountable to each other in your Christian walk and develop an exemplary Christian character.

1. Have you been a good example this week to of your transformation in Jesus Christ with both your words and actions?
2. Have you been involved in any way with sexually alluring material or allowed your mind to entertain inappropriate sexual thoughts about another this week?
3. Have you lacked integrity in your financial dealings or coveted something that does not belong to you?
4. Have you been honoring, understanding, and generous in your important relationships this week?
5. Have you damaged another person by your words, either behind their back or face-to-face?
6. Have you given in to an addictive behavior this past week? Explain.
7. Have you remained angry toward another?
8. Have you secretly wished for another's misfortune so you might excel?
9. Did you finish your Bible reading for group this week and hear from God? What are you going to do about it?
10. Have you been completely honest with yourself and your accountability partner?

ACCEPTING JESUS

There is a first time that each of us first encounter Jesus. You might have met Jesus many years ago, or it is possible you met Him and did not even realize it was Him. Half the world dies without ever knowing about Jesus. Along many people's everyday journey through life, they meet Jesus for the first time. It might be through a good deed, a book, a friend, or even a crisis. When the original twelve disciples met Jesus, they were working their daily jobs as fishermen. Once you meet Jesus, you must either accept or reject Him, as there is no middle ground on which to stand. For some, it takes their entire life to follow Him and for others only the time it takes to speak His name.

The first disciples were Jews and taught from a young age of the coming Christ, the Messiah. Even waiting years for Jesus to come it took many, time to accept that Jesus was in person amongst them. The first disciples met Jesus on an ordinary day. He walked up to them and asked them to follow Him. To be a disciple, you must first accept to follow Jesus as the Messiah.

A good place to learn more about Jesus and the good news He brought into the world is to start with the book of John in the Bible. Those who have accepted Jesus may have never committed to learning more of Him than what others have told them. The book of John is a great introduction to Jesus and His life.

Listen to your heart as you read; what is it saying to you? Ask Jesus to show you He is the Son of God and make that real to you. If you want to meet Jesus and settle it in your heart once-and-for-always, He will show you He is the Christ. Remember, He made you, knows you, and has been pursuing you since the day of your birth. He's been pursuing each of us since the day He created Adam and Eve in the garden.

Jesus, the Son of God died for your sins, rose from death on the third day, and will forgive you of your sins. The Bible says to be saved, a person must, "...repent and be baptized for the forgiveness of your sins" (Acts 2:38). Then you must put your trust in Jesus Christ and believe in Him, and you will be saved (Acts 16:31).

If you're ready to give your life to Jesus, start by repenting for your sins. Tell Him you are sorry for your sins and thank Him for giving His life on the cross for you. Tell Him you believe He rose to life on the third day, and He has saved you from your sins and death and that He has given you eternal life. Repent of your sins and begin trusting in Jesus and your salvation from eternity in Hell is secure. Find another Christian who can baptize you whether it be in the ocean, pool, or church.

It is that simple to accept Jesus, acknowledge that He is the creator of the universe and you, and start living your life with purpose. It is by faith that we believe in Jesus, and through that faith we are born again. Now, as we read in 1 Peter, we are "born again to a living hope through the resurrection of Jesus Christ from the dead, to an inheritance that is imperishable, undefiled, and unfading, kept in heaven for you, who by God's power are being guarded through faith for a salvation ready to be revealed in the last time" (1 Peter 1:3-5 ESV). Nothing and no one can take that gift of eternal life away from you. It doesn't mean your life gets easier; many of the disciples found there were more challenges to life. Jesus will transform your life like the disciples, giving it purpose, and use you to tell others of Him.

Once you accept Jesus, there is only one thing left to do, follow Him, and make disciples.

Taken from *Ancient Paths, Untangling the Complexity of Discipleship*, Scott Michael Ringo

NOTES

one

1. Unless otherwise noted, all biblical passages referenced are in the English Standard Version.

ABOUT THE AUTHOR

Scott Michael Ringo is a seasoned author who writes from his experience around the world. Scott has had the fortune in life to be as the ancient explorers, living life at its fullest and always curiously looking down the unexplored, overgrown trails that lead to new beauty. Jumping aboard a schooner bound for the open sea or charting an island that needs finding, full of riches in every turn. Join with Scott and explore and discover this amazing world that God created for us to live our life glorifying Him by making disciples, while being in an intimate relationship with our passionate lover, Jesus.

TITLES BY SCOTT MICHAEL RINGO

Ancient Paths, Untangling the Complexity of Discipleship

Coffee For One, Daily Devotions that Inspire

Transform, Transformed by Our Encounter with Jesus

Simple Fundraising, Easy Non-Profit Fundraising

Explosive Marketing

Simple Non-Profit Fundraising